WORLDWIDE ADVENTURE

SOCIETY

THE
ADVENTURES OF

Lily Huckleberry
in
Scandinavia

by

AUDREY SMIT & JACKIE KNAPP

ISBN: 978-1-7326961-1-2

The Adventures of Lily Huckleberry in Scandinavia is available at special quantity discounts for bulk purchase for wholesale, fundraising, and educational needs.
For details, write to wholesale@thislittlestreet.com

Story by Audrey Smit & Jackie Knapp.
Words by Jackie & illustrations by Audrey.
Editor: Mick Silva
Visual Consultant: Juliet Meeks

Artwork on page 52-53 is "Efter Massakern, Study from North Norway" by Swedish artist Anna Boberg, date unknown. Via National Museum of Sweden. Public domain.

Printed in China.

The Adventures of Lily Huckleberry is FSC certified. It is printed on chlorine-free paper made with 30% post-consumer waste.
It uses only vegetable and soy-based ink.

Published by This Little Street ™
www.thislittlestreet.com

Follow @lilyhuckleberry and @thislittlestreet
on Instagram

Second Edition
10 9 8 7 6 5 4 3 2

HI FRIENDS,
CHECK PAGE 92 FOR A LITTLE
SURPRISE FROM ME!

TO THE CURIOUS,
THE WANDERERS,
THE FREE SPIRITS
LOOKING FOR ADVENTURE...

THIS STORY IS FOR YOU.

In a village where the flowers grow as big as trees,
lives a girl named Lily Huckleberry.

Lily lives on a little street, in the yellow house with the
heart on the door. Her little street is a funny place. Silly really.

The mothers camp in tree houses and the fathers jump in puddles, and
the old man in the green house eats ice cream for breakfast every day.

And every morning, Lily dances to the end of the street, throws her arms in the air, and yells,

"GOOD MORNING BEAUTIFUL WORLD!
I'M READY FOR YOU!"

You should try it, especially if you are grumpy in the mornings.

One day, Lily noticed a girl walking down her street.

"Hello, I'm Lily!"

"I'm Freia, and I'm from Scandinavia."

"Scandinavia? Is that a magical candy land?"

"No, silly Lily. Scandinavia is Denmark, Sweden, and Norway, up north in the sea."

"Why do you have flowers in your hair?" Lily asked.

"It's almost Midsummer, the time for our big party to celebrate the light, because it's dark for so long in winter. We wear flower crowns, eat strawberry cake, and dance around a maypole."

"Ooooh! I want to go to that party! I love dancing. And strawberry cake!"

Lily and Freia played all day, and Freia gave Lily some of her salty licorice. Lily wrinkled her nose, "this candy tastes like the sea!"

At the end of the day, Freia hugged Lily good-bye. Lily cried. "You are my first friend from Scandinavia, please don't leave!"

"Don't cry, silly Lily! Run home...there is a surprise on your doorstep!"

Lily ran home and found a globe with a big green ribbon.
And a note.

DEAR LILY,

BECAUSE OF YOUR CURIOUS SPIRIT, WE, THE WORLDWIDE ADVENTURE SOCIETY OF SHENANIGANS AND HULLABALOOS, HEREBY INVITE YOU TO JOIN OUR SOCIETY.

MEMBERS ARE REQUIRED TO BE:
1. VERY SILLY
2. VERY BRAVE
3. ALWAYS READY FOR ADVENTURE

<u>NOT</u> ALLOWED:
1. STICKS-IN-THE-MUD
2. FUN TAKERS
3. MAGIC DOUBTERS

OFFICIAL

IF YOU ACCEPT, PLEASE READ THE GLOBE FOR INSTRUCTIONS TO BEGIN YOUR MAGICAL HULLABALOOS.

ADVENTURES AWAIT,
YOUR FRIENDS AT THE SOCIETY

Lily was so excited she ran around the room
17 times until she fell over laughing.

"I've never been part of a secret society before!
Beautiful world, I'm ready for you!"

She twirled the globe around until she found Scandinavia.
Was the globe really magical?

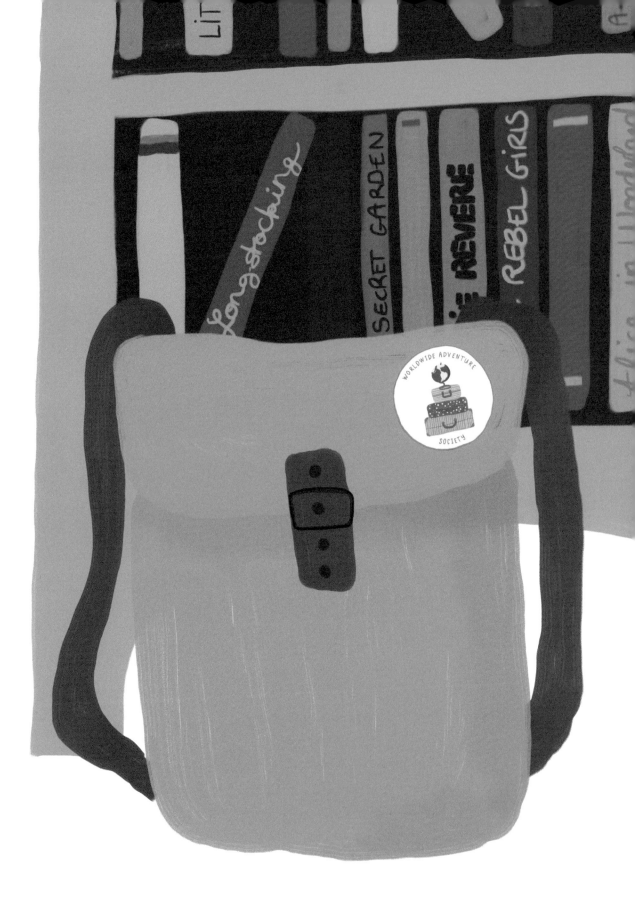

Lily read the tag:

Adventures await,
if you close your eyes & shout

GOODBYE COLLY WOBBLES,
GOODBYE BELLY BOBBLES!
TIME FOR BALLYHOO!
TAKE ME TO A HULLABALOO!

So Lily closed her eyes and tried.

"Dear Globe, I want to go to Scandinavia and the Midsummer party.
So, goodbye wobble cobbles, uh, hobbles dobbles....
Oh. My belly must have bobbles, I can't get it right!"

Could you say it with her? That might help.

"GOODBYE COLLY WOBBLES, GOODBYE BELLY BOBBLES!
TIME FOR BALLYHOO! TAKE ME TO A HULLABALOO!"

When she opened her eyes, all she could see were flowers, flowers everywhere, and two feet in red shoes and stripy socks.

Peeking out of the flowers was...

Freia!

"You're here, Lily Huckleberry! Welcome to Denmark, and my Midsummer party!"

They skipped around the meadow, meeting all of Freia's friends.

"Oh, I almost forgot! We need to help my mormor," Freia said.

"Who?" Lily asked.   [MORE-MORE]

"My grandma. She's making the strawberry cake."

Mel

Sukker

Mormor clapped her hands.
"Welcome, Lily!"

They stirred the batter until Mormor yelped, "Oh, NEJ!
The strawberries are gone!
This will ruin Midsummer!"

[N-EYE]

Lily jumped up. "I can go find some, Mormor!"

Mormor sighed. "It may be hard, Lily. The berry patch is tricky to find."

"Easy peasy, Mormor. Remember, my name is
Lily HuckleBERRY– no berry can hide from me!"

Lily found the sign tree like Mormor had told her, but it was confusing. Danish had funny letters she didn't know.

For the first time, Lily Huckleberry felt very far from home.

Let's help Lily.

Can you find the sign for the berry patch?

Lily found the patch, but no berries!
Just then, she heard a sneaky giggle.
She looked around to find the gigglebox.

"Gilly Lily! Over here, over here! Look down, dilly willy!!
Don't step on Mr. Nisse." [NISS-UH]

"You look like a friend, Mr. Nisse. Can you help me? I'm stuck!"

"Stuck in the muck like a duck. Quack, quack!" He waddled in a circle.

Lily giggled at the strange little elf.

"What am I going to do? I told Mormor this was easy-peasy!"

"The likings of the Vikings took the berries on their ferries."

"What?"

"Go to pretty city Copenhagen for your merry berries."

"Vikings? Aren't they mean?"

Mr. Nisse nodded and pointed to the path. "Good luck, stuck duck."

Then he flapped into the bushes with a "quack, quack!"

Lily's belly bobbled, but she kept walking.
The forest felt like a fairy tale.

Soon enough, there it was: Copenhagen!

The flowers waved and the horses neighed.

Lily hopped through the sweet, green grass.

"How could the Vikings steal
anything in such a happy place?"
Lily wondered.

Copenhagen was much bigger than Lily's little street. She twirled
on the cobblestone streets, peeking in the shops and windows.

It smelled like summer and ice cream,
and as the bikes whizzed past her, Lily couldn't stop smiling.

She danced down the street and yelled,

"HELLO BEAUTIFUL WORLD! I'M READY FOR YOU!"

At the ice cream shop, the ice cream man asked her
if she wanted marshmallow guf on her cone.

[GOOF]

Lily giggled. "Goof? Yes, please, I'll have goof, you goof!"

She asked if he had any strawberries. He shook his head sadly and pointed to the colorful harbor. "Try the market at Nyhavn."

[NU-HAWN]

But when Lily got to the market....no strawberries!

"What a crazy day!" the shopkeeper said.
"Some big guys with horns took them when I wasn't looking!"

"Oh no!" Lily said. She knew exactly who had taken them.

"Maybe The Little Mermaid can help? She's great in nautical disasters."

The shopkeeper pointed to the end of the pier.

The Little Mermaid! Lily's eyes grew as big as the sea.

At the end of the pier, Lily found a real mermaid!
"Did you see the Vikings?"

"Yes! Their ship went toward Sweden, across this sea.
Do you want to go for a swim?"

Lily nodded but there were bobbles in her belly.

This was turning into a very big adventure!
She'd just passed her swimming test,
but she'd never swum to another country with a mermaid.

Then she remembered her adventure words.
Can you say them with her?

"GOODBYE COLLYWOBBLES,
GOODBYE BELLY BOBBLES!
TIME FOR BALLYHOO!
TAKE ME TO A HULLABALOO!"

And she jumped into
the cold, cold sea.

Lily didn't think she could swim all the way to Sweden, but her new friend taught her to kick like a mermaid.

They somersaulted with the fish and played
hide and seek with her mermaid friends.

[MAL-MUH]

In Malmö, Sweden, they spotted Viking tracks, but no Vikings.

"I know! The queen's mice spies live here!
Their headquarters are right around the corner.
Ask them what they know about this Viking situation."

Before Lily could reply, her friend dove away.

Lily scratched her head.

Mice spies? Scandinavia was a very silly place.

Lily walked around the corner and saw a tiny tail squeeze through a tiny door. She bent down and knocked quietly.

Two black eyes peered at her.

"Code, please."

"Uh, my name is Lily Huckleberry," she stammered.
"We have a Viking situation!"

The door flew open, and a mouse leapt out. "Magnus Melker, at your service." He held out a tiny cake. "Eat this so you can come inside."

Lily loved cake, but she wasn't sure about cake from spies.

"Hurry!" Mag urged.

Lily shrugged and swallowed the cake.
A few seconds later she was mouse-size.

"Holy-moly, I'm teeny-tiny!" Mag pulled her inside.

Smart-looking mice
gathered around a table
with sweets and warm drinks.

[FEE-KA]

"Fika?" Mag asked.
"It's our coffee break."

"Yes, please!"

Mag said Viking situations
made him extra hungry,
so he ate 13 cinnamon buns
and drank 11 cups of coffee.

The mice pulled out their
Viking Tracker 4000 and
began searching for Vikings.

"Oh, this is more than a
situation!" Mag groaned.

"There is not a SINGLE
strawberry left in ALL of
Scandinavia! Midsummer is
hanging by a thread. This is
a CODE BERRY, people!"

"The queen must be warned!
Take her this report." Mag said.
"Use our secret tunnel, Lily!"

Before she could blink,
Lily was sliding down
a swirly-twirly tunnel.

"Wheeeeeeee!"
Lily shouted.

PLOP!

Lily landed in the
castle, people-size again.

She gave the report to
Queen Silvia and tried
to curtsey.

The king asked Lily if
she wanted to try
his new chair, but the
queen gasped as
she read the report.

"There's no time for sitting!
We must help Lily
save Midsummer! Come!"

Queen Silvia brought Lily a magnificent horse.

"This is Dala who will take you to Thorsen, the strongest guy
in all of Scandinavia. He once lifted 72 reindeer over a mountain!
Thorsen isn't afraid of those Vikings! Are you ready, Lily Huckleberry?"

Lily curtsied again. "Easy-peasy, your majesty."

This time, she didn't even feel the bobbles.

As they galloped away from the palace, Dala bellowed,

"FOR SWEDEN AND HER BERRIES!
ONWARD MY LADY, ONWARD!"

They flew through the flowers and Lily wondered,
"Dala, are you a unicorn?"

Dala sighed. "Miss Lily, do you see a horn on my head? Don't get me wrong, I love those guys, but I'm my own kind of Swedish magic."

Lily patted him, "You are magic, Dala."

Dala raced through the
enchanted forest.

And lickety-split, they came to a village.

"Welcome to Norway, Miss Lily."

"What is this place, Dala?" Lily asked.

"This is Thorsen's fjord." [FEE-YORD]

"The mountains and the sea are all mixed together!"

Lily felt mouse-size again.

"Fjords are the most magical place on earth. Anything is possible here."
Dala nuzzled her. "You are brave, Lily Huckleberry."

"You're my best magic horse, Dala," she said, sliding down.

Lily tiptoed to the red cabin, not feeling very brave.

The collywobbles were back.

What if Thorsen was a meanie?

She used
all her
muscles to
knock on
the door.

"Lily Huckleberry?" a gruff voice asked.

"Yes, sir?" Lily squeaked.

The door creaked open and a man towered over her, the biggest man Lily had ever seen.

"They told me they were sending you on that old unicorn."

"He's not a unicorn!"

Thorsen winked, then burst into laughter.

"I know, I just love to tease him.

Come on in, Huckleberry!"

Thorsen's house was bright and cozy.

Lily looked around, "You like flowers? I didn't think a tough guy like you would like flowers."

"People aren't always what they seem. Never forget that, Huckleberry."

Lily and Thorsen both loved knock-knock jokes, and spent their dinner giggling at each other.

"Thorsen, did you really lift 72 reindeer? I thought reindeer could fly."

"I can't tell you all my secrets," he winked at her. "But I will tell you about the Vikings. Now, eat up, we have a big climb ahead of us!"

Lily and Thorsen started the climb to find the Vikings.

"Are we there yet?" Lily's feet whined and whined.

"You'll be a real Norwegian after a hike like this! Only 14 miles to go!"

Lily thought they would never get to the top.

As they reached the top of the fjord,
Lily shouted, "we're flying, Thorsen!"

She peered over the cliff.
"I can see the Viking ship!
And the strawberries! We did it!"

Thorsen winked at her and they
danced a little jig, on top of the world.

"How do we get down there?"

"Close your eyes," Thorsen said. "I have a surprise."

When Lily opened her eyes, a sparkly rainbow bridge
stretched down to the village.

"WOW!! Is that for me?"

Thorsen nodded. "But I'm afraid I can't come with you.
You'll have to go talk to the Vikings alone."

Lily felt the bobbles rushing back, and the collywobbles too!

She squeezed his big hand. "I'm scared, Thorsen."

"If anyone can save Midsummer, you're the one," he said.

"You were born for adventure, Huckleberry!"

Lily took a deep breath, and shouted,

"FOR SCANDINAVIA AND HER BERRIES!"

And she jumped.

KER-SPLAT! Lily landed at the end of the rainbow in a heap.

The Vikings stared down at her. Lily stumbled to her feet.

"Who are you?" a woman with one big eyebrow barked.

Lily tried to find her voice. "I'm Lily Huckleberry. Who are you?"

"I'm Dagmar. What are you doing here?"

"Umm... I'm wondering why you're stealing strawberries."

"If you must know, we're angry!" Dagmar said.

"We're not allowed at Midsummer parties because we used to be very bad. But we've been good for so long. Look at our report card!"

REPORT CARD
Name: VIKINGS

GOOD JOB

Pillaging free:
952 years
7 months
and 181 days

MOST IMPROVED!

A+

"We took all the strawberries, so no one could have fun!"

Suddenly, one of the Vikings began to cry!

"Waah! Waah! I've been dreaming about my flower crown, and now I don't get to make one! It's my only dream!" Troels cried and cried.

Lily stood in a puddle of Viking tears.

Thorsen was right. People aren't always what they seem.

"Please don't cry," Lily said. "You know that stealing is no way to make friends, right?"

The Vikings shook their heads. "We're not good at making friends, Lily Huckleberry."

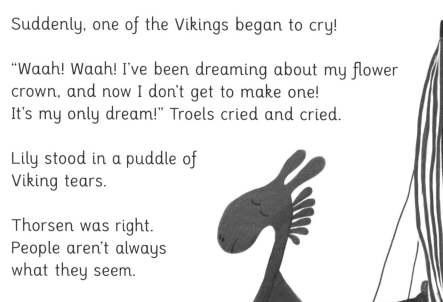

Just then, Lily got an idea. "Freia will let you come to her party!
I'll teach you how to make friends on the way."
Troels smiled through his tears. "You would do that?"

"Let's go!" Dagmar said. And all the Vikings cheered!

"ALL ABOARD THE DRAGON SHIP!"

They picked up some friends and chased the midnight sun. The Vikings let Lily ride on the top of the dragon's head so she could be the teacher.

"Okay, Vikings. Repeat after me!"

"I WILL NOT BURN DOWN ANY HOUSES."
"I WILL NOT PICK FIGHTS WITH ANYONE."
"I WILL NOT STEAL (EVEN STRAWBERRIES)."
"I WILL BE A FRIEND TO MAKE FRIENDS."

"Good Vikings!"
Lily beamed at her students.

Back in
Denmark, Freia was waiting.

"Freia, can the Vikings come to the party?
We were wrong about them! They are
ready to be friends, not fighters."

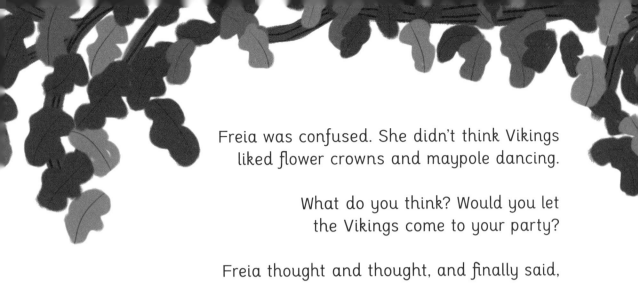

Freia was confused. She didn't think Vikings
liked flower crowns and maypole dancing.

What do you think? Would you let
the Vikings come to your party?

Freia thought and thought, and finally said,
"Let's do second chances! Welcome to our party, Vikings."

The happy Vikings skipped around the meadow,
helping set up the party.

Freia showed Troels how to make his flower crown,
and he heaped the strawberries into a
lovely pile on top of the cake.

Everyone danced around the maypole
until they could dance no more
and ate strawberry cake until
their bellies burst.

It was more magical than
Lily had imagined.

At the end of the party, Freia gathered everyone together.

"Lily Huckleberry, you were very brave on this adventure!
On behalf of the Society, here is a patch
to remember your Scandinavian hullabaloo!"

Lily squealed and twirled around "Thanks, friends!
It was a berry good adventure, Scandinavia!

Now, where should I go next?"

— The End

NORTH
SEA

NORWAY

SWEDEN

Oslo

STOCKHOLM

DENMARK

COPENHAGEN

BALTIC
SEA

SCANDINAVIAN
Hidden treasures!

THE PEOPLE OF SCANDINAVIA LOVE TO SHOW THEIR FLAGS. CAN YOU REMEMBER WHICH ONE IS FOR WHICH COUNTRY?

The Vikings worshipped the Norse gods, including Thor, God of Thunder & his mighty hammer. Did you see a hammer in the story?

The Little Mermaid was written by Danish writer Hans Christian Andersen. There are nine more of his fairy tales hidden in the forest on pages 30-31. How many can you find?

Answer: The Ugly Duckling The Emperor's New Clothes, The Snow Queen, Thumbelina, The Nightingale, The Tinderbox, The Beetle Who Went on His travels, The Butterfly, The Teapot

WE HID THE NATIONAL BIRDS OF EACH COUNTRY IN THE BOOK!

DENMARK = SWAN
SWEDEN = BLACK BIRD
NORWAY = WHITE-THROATED DIPPER.

DID YOU SEE THEM?

THE METRO STATIONS OF STOCKHOLM, SWEDEN ARE PAINTED WITH MANY COLORS AND DESIGNS, WHICH INSPIRED OUR MOUSE TUNNEL!

An artist collective named Anonymouse MMX actually creates mouse restaurants and shops (like our mice spy headquarters) around Malmö, Sweden and other cities!

Scandinavia is world-known for its beautiful furniture design. We hid some in the book, did you find them?

SOME OF THE FLAVORS SCANDINAVIANS LOVE THE MOST ARE BERRIES, RHUBARB, ELDERFLOWER, FISH, SWEETS, BLACK BREAD, AND SALTY THINGS (LIKE FREIA'S CANDY). CAN YOU FIND EACH ONE IN THE BOOK?

Lily's rainbow bridge is a wink to Norse mythology. In those legends, a rainbow bridge called Bifrost is believed to connect the land of humans and the land of gods.

Scandinavia...did you know?

BIKES: The people of Scandinavia love biking. In Copenhagen, it is common for people to bike to work, rain or shine. There are twice as many bikes as there are cars in Denmark!

BUNADS: The people of Norway wear bunads, the traditional dress in the colors of the Norwegian flag for weddings and celebrations. Find the bunads on page 60.

CASTLE: The castle Lily visits is Drottningholm Palace in Stockholm, Sweden. It is only one of the Swedish royal family's 11 castles!

DALA horses are colorful painted wooden horses, originally from the province of Dalarna in Sweden. Don't mix them up with unicorns!

FIKA is Swedish for a coffee and cake break. It includes warm drinks, sweets, and friends!

FJORD: Thorsen's fjord was inspired by Trolltunga, Norway. The majestic cliff stands over 2,000 feet high!

HYGGE (hoo-gah) means the feeling of coziness, which is very important to Scandinavian culture. There are many ways to experience hygge, including candles, blankets, and meals shared with friends. See if you can find hygge in the pictures!

LITTLE MERMAID: Her statue sits on a rock in the waterfront of Copenhagen, Denmark. Look carefully in the water, she may be smaller than you expect!

MORMOR: Maternal and paternal grandparents have different names in Scandinavia! Mormor = mom's mom I Morfar = mom's dad I Farmor = dad's mom I Farfar = dad's dad.

MIDSUMMER is celebrated every year around summer solstice, which is the third week in June. Each region of Scandinavia celebrates its own special way.

NISSE: Mr. Nisse would normally come around Christmas. Nisse are elves who are sometimes helpful and sometimes naughty. They are called tomte in Sweden.

NYHAVN is a famous harbor in Copenhagen. Although it means "new harbor," it was built in the 17th century.

ØRESUND BRIDGE links Denmark and Sweden. It is nearly 5 miles (8 km) long! You can see it on the page where Lily swims with the mermaid to Sweden.

QUEEN: Denmark, Norway and Sweden are all kingdoms, which means that they are ruled by a king and/or Queen, like King Carl and Queen Silvia of Sweden.

REINDEER: Reindeer are still herded in the the far north of Scandinavia by the Sami people. These guys don't work for Santa Claus. Or do they?

SCANDINAVIA: Scandinavia is made up of Denmark, Norway & Sweden. Add Iceland and Finland to the mix and you have the Nordic countries.

VIKINGS: The last Viking raid happened in 1066, but the Viking culture still influences Scandinavia today.

HI FRIENDS,

HOLY-MOLY! THAT WAS A VERY BIG ADVENTURE, AND I'M SO GLAD YOU CAME ALONG! WHAT WAS YOUR FAVORITE PART?

I CAN'T STOP DREAMING ABOUT WHERE I'LL GO NEXT. WHAT DO YOU THINK? JAPAN? COSTA RICA? KEEP SAILING WITH THE VIKINGS?

PLEASE SEND ME YOUR IDEAS, PICTURES AND STORIES FROM YOUR ADVENTURES. HERE IS MY ADDRESS:

> LILY HUCKLEBERRY
> THIS LITTLE STREET
> PO BOX 7630
> BERKELEY, CA 94707

> OR EMAIL ME ON THE COMPUTER!
> LILYHUCKLEBERRY@THISLITTLESTREET.COM

EASY-PEASY! MAKE SURE TO WRITE YOUR ADDRESS, SO I CAN SEND YOU A SURPRISE FROM THE WORLDWIDE ADVENTURE SOCIETY!

I LOVE MAKING NEW FRIENDS. I CAN'T WAIT TO GET YOUR NOTES!

> ADVENTURES AWAIT!
> LOVE,
>
> Lily

A note from the authors

Sometimes, ideas become things. What started as a casual conversation over a year ago has blossomed into a book. It still feels a bit magical, just like Lily's adventure.

We've loved working on this project, spending many hours at the kitchen table unearthing the charm and beauty of Scandinavian culture. Also laughing for hours while meticulously compiling a Silly Word Database.

Once we realized we had indeed written a book, we took our own leap of faith and launched a Kickstarter campaign. An incredible community emerged overnight, and we fully funded in six days. That night, we danced around the same kitchen table, in awe that we were going to be able to publish Lily's adventure ourselves.

Thank you for being brave enough to take a risk on us, coming along for the hullabaloo. We hope Lily's stories inspire you and your little ones to embrace whimsy, creativity, and courage, to find the adventure in the everyday. We think there is nothing better than exploring the unknown and making new friends!

A huge thank you to our friends and family who cheered us on, read countless drafts, endured rainy photoshoots, grew out beards and never stopped believing these adventures would come to life. We love you!

From the bottom of our berry loving hearts,

Jackie + Audrey

AUDREY SMIT is the founder of This Little Street, a design company with a colorful and happy aesthetic. A pattern designer and illustrator, Audrey desires This Little Street to be driven by meaningful stories to build a colorful world where kids can dream, discover and learn. Originally from France, Audrey lives in Berkeley, CA with her Danish husband and their four silly, adventurous little girls, who give her a good run for her money and are constant sources of inspiration for her work.

FOLLOW HER ON INSTAGRAM @THISLITTLESTREET

JACKIE KNAPP wrote her first story about talking animals in the 2nd grade. For the past two decades, she has mentored and taught kids worldwide, recently working with orphans in Liberia. She serves as a Children's Ministry Director in Albany, CA, developing a creative arts program that empowers children to collaborate on original films. Jackie has degrees in counseling and psychology, and believes that the stories kids read shape the adults they become. This is her first children's series, inspired by a Thursday Adventure Club concocted for Audrey's girls and her own gypsy spirit.

FOLLOW HER ON INSTAGRAM @GYPSYJAC

Connect with us @LILYHUCKLEBERRY on Instagram.
Or drop us a line: LILYHUCKLEBERRY@THISLITTLESTREET.COM

We would love to hear from you!